Bulbul Sharma is a writer and an artist. She teaches art to children with special needs. She is the author of a number of books for adults and children. She lives mostly in the hills where she loves going on bird-watching and talking-to-trees excursions.

# Birds in My Garden and Beyond

Bulbul Sharma

talking CUB

An Imprint of Speaking Tiger Books

TALKING CUB
Published by Speaking Tiger Books LLP
125 A Ground Floor, Shahpur Jat, Near Asiad Village
New Delhi–110049, India

Published in Talking Cub by Speaking Tiger Books in paperback in 2020
First published by Indus, an imprint of HarperCollins Publishers, in India in 1991



ISBN:
eISBN:

10 9 8 7 6 5 4 3 2 1



Book design by Maithili Doshi Aphale
Typset in Adobe Garamond Pro by Jojy Philip
Printed at Sanat Printers, Kundli

*For my grandchildren Naina, Shivam,*
*Samara, Prithvi and Shiv*

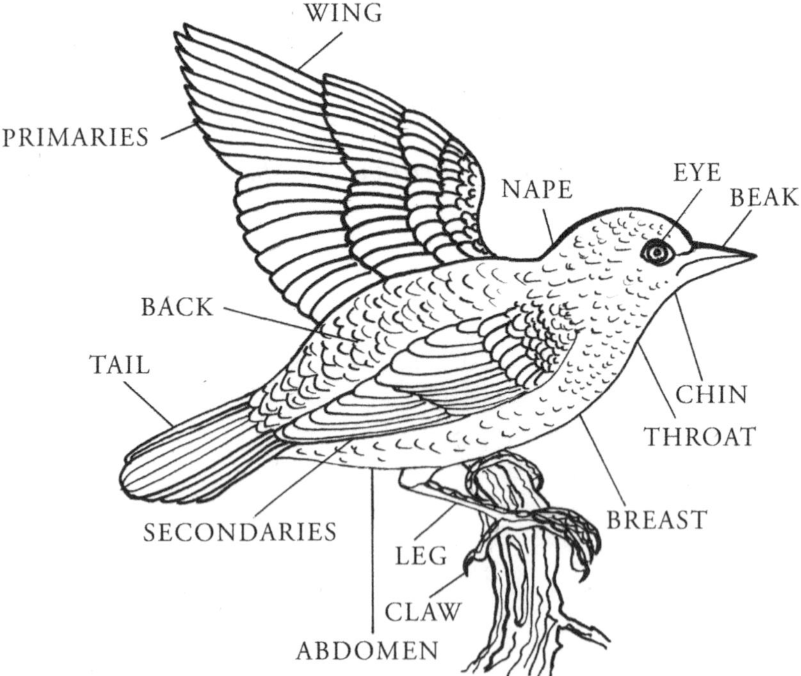
WING
PRIMARIES
NAPE
EYE
BEAK
BACK
TAIL
CHIN
THROAT
BREAST
SECONDARIES
LEG
CLAW
ABDOMEN

# Chapter One

*The sparrows had spotted the enemy* prowling around the jamun tree. All of them started calling out together, hopping up and down on their tiny legs. The cat, a plump black and yellow one with a torn ear and lots of attitude, ignored them and began to dig in the wet mud. I wondered why he was doing that. As I walked out of the garden, I

saw the sparrows flying around in an agitated way, chirping loudly. The cat was still digging with a naughty grin on his face. Cats can grin, you know, at least this one does, just to annoy the birds in my garden.

Every morning all kinds of little squabbles take place in my garden as the

birds arrive one by one. The garden has many old trees and shrubs and is quite wild, so the birds love it. They can find plenty to eat in the shrubs and there is always lots of useful nesting materials like twigs, old wool (from my knitting bag), dried grass and leaves to be found here. From early morning till dusk, when the light fades, you can hear birds singing, chattering or arguing in my garden. I wish I knew what they were saying. Don't you?

If I could understand their language

of melodious tones, shrill calls and low chattering, I would know exactly what they were saying to each other. Shall we try and guess?

Look, here is the purple sunbird, hovering in front of the bright red hibiscus flower. She is squeaking in a soft voice and probably complaining that there is not enough juice in the flower this morning.

Most flowers contain a sweet juice called nectar, which is the favourite drink of many birds. The purple sunbird is a tiny bird with shiny blue-black feathers and a sharp pointed beak. This beak is useful for sipping nectar from flowers and also picking up tiny insects.

A black-and-white magpie robin singing loudly flies in and tries to scare the purple sunbird away by saying a few rude words. When that does not work, it begins to sing a beautiful tune: 'Tweee… swee…twee…' The bird whistles to announce the nectar is sweet.

The birds often have to share the nectar from the flowers with butterflies. The butterflies usually come out on sunny days and spend a long time gliding around on their beautiful wings. They take care to stay away from the birds

since some of them might just catch them for their breakfast. Did you know that some butterflies mimic the wing patterns and colours of other butterflies that are poisonous so that the birds do not eat them? What a clever thing to do.

Here comes the hoopoe calling out its own name loudly over and over again till it is sure you have heard it. I often see

this bird with black-and-white zebra-striped wings running up and down the garden in a great hurry as if trying to catch a bus. Actually, the bird is only looking for a few juicy worms that it can dig out from the earth with its long, pointed beak. The hoopoe has a jaunty, smart crest, that it usually keeps neatly

folded but may suddenly surprise you by flicking it open like a paper fan.

Another bird that cannot stop talking is the dumpy little coppersmith. She sits on a leafy branch and calls out 'tuk-tuk-tuk' all through the day. She has a funny way of bobbing her head up and down as she calls, as if to show off the tiny red cap she wears on her head. When the peepal tree in the garden is full of tiny fruits, I can hear at least four coppersmiths going 'tuk-tuk-tuk' all day.

The golden oriole flies in but hides

shyly among the green leaves of the peepal tree. When he gives a low, musical whistle you can catch a glimpse of his bright yellow feathers.

The morning sun is now right on top of our heads and the cat has gone for his afternoon nap after finishing his mysterious digging. I can hear the bulbuls chattering from the jamun tree. I think they are asking each other what the cat was up to. Was he digging a tunnel? Was he searching for hidden treasure?

The dark brown red-vented bulbul and its cousin the red-whiskered bulbul chat all day and sing loudly from the jamun tree. These noisy birds are seen everywhere in the garden and also in parks, chasing away any other bird that tries to come near their territory. They eat insects, berries and drink nectar from flowers and never stop their chattering.

There are some shady spots in the garden and the squirrels

like to rest in these cool corners during the afternoon. I sometimes see the cat watching them from his own cool place but so far he has never been able to catch even one since the squirrels are much

faster than the fat cat. These furry, long-tailed creatures make a squeaky noise that sounds like a bird chattering. They build untidy nests with bits of paper, grass and string.

The tiny tailorbird can never live in such an untidy nest and builds a neat little home for itself. The bird has a sharp beak that has a pointed tip. This clever bird uses the beak to stitch up leaves into a nest. First it selects large, droopy-looking leaves, then, without breaking off the leaf from the stem, it folds them and makes tiny holes along the edges. Now the tailorbird shows off its skills and stitches the leaves using fine thread it has collected from the garden. When this leaf cone is ready, the bird makes a small cup out of cotton wool and soft fibres. This comfy-looking cup is placed right in the middle of the leaf cone.

Once the tailorbird's nest is ready, it looks just like the other leaf bunches up on the branch and it is very difficult to spot where the nest is. This way the nest is safe from enemies like cats, rats and

crows and they cannot steal the tailorbird's eggs or chicks. Smaller birds always have to be careful about hiding their nests. You will notice that they never land right on their nests, in case some enemy is watching them. The birds will hop on the branch above or below the nest and then fly home when they are sure there are no suspicious strangers around. The tailorbird has a

very loud call for such a tiny bird. You may be able to find its nest if you try to listen where the call is coming from.

You can never miss the bright green rose-ringed parakeets in the garden because they never sit quietly in one place and love flying around screeching

loudly. They eat fruits and flower buds and nest in holes in tree trunks. You will often see a green head and an orange-red beak peeping out of tree hollows. They are very fond of old ruins and sometimes make their homes in these monuments. People catch these pretty birds and put them in cages. Then they do not look so happy. If I could understand what they are saying, I am sure I would find that they are complaining about us.

The little brown dove is not noisy like the parakeets. This gentle bird has

become the symbol of peace all over the world. I hear it calling 'coo roo…cooo' in its soft voice during the summer afternoons. The dove eats seeds and grains and walks in a funny, zigzag manner on the ground searching for fallen seeds,

cooing to itself happily. Though doves are always good tempered and friendly, they can put up a brave fight if other birds try to attack their nest.

House sparrows are the most friendly birds in my garden. They come and sit by the kitchen, chattering noisily with each other as they wait for the rice grains I usually scatter for them. They are not

afraid of the fat cat and sometimes jump dangerously close to his greedy jaws. Sparrows were once very common in the gardens and parks but now they are getting fewer. They prefer to live inside a house than in the garden. You may have seen sparrows nesting on ceiling fans and lamp shades. Do you think that is why they are called house sparrows?

Another bird that loves the sound of its own voice is the common blue rock pigeon. All day long you can hear it saying to itself 'gooter-goo gooter-goo' then as if impressed with what it has said it will reply quickly with another 'guterr…gutterrrrr'. These birds, like sparrows, love living near us and feed on grains and seeds. They always perch on statues in a park and make quite a mess. The mother pigeon feeds her chicks in an unusual way. She has a special sac in her neck and the chicks can drink a kind

of milk from it. There is another kind of pigeon that lives amongst the leaves on the higher branches of a tree and calls in a soft, musical voice. This plump, green bird is called a green pigeon. It loves only fruits and berries and you very rarely see it mixing with its cousin on the ground.

The mynas, you must have seen everywhere, greedily eating whatever they can find. They love picking a quarrel with other birds and ruffle everyone's feathers for no reason at all. Some kinds of mynas and parakeets can learn to mimic the speech of humans.

The crows are greedy too and very clever at picking up leftover food. Eagles, kites, vultures and crows are not fussy about what they eat and they help us by eating up all the rotting and dead animals. They are called scavenging birds.

The snails and earthworms that crawl slowly on the ground and take almost all day to reach from one place to another, also help us by turning up the soil and letting it breathe. Snails are often eaten by bigger birds that crush their shells by banging them against a stone. There are spiders too living quietly amongst the plants, secretly trapping insects in their silky webs. A spider makes a web out of silken threads that it spins out of its own body. What fun if you too could spin the yarn yourself and make yourself a soft T-shirt!

Spiders, snails, earthworms and butterflies have to be very careful as they go around the garden since all the insect-eating birds are just waiting to catch them and gobble them up. These secret battles carry on all day in the garden and you may never even get to see these fights. It is only when the cat attacks the mynas or sparrows that I get to know what is going on since they make a huge racket. But the cat never manages to catch a single bird. He always

retires hurt to a corner and glares at the happy birds, thinking dark thoughts.

You may see a group of six or seven birds having a great time hopping on the ground and chatting away. They are jungle babblers. These brownish-grey

birds love to hang out together and share whatever food they find in the soil.

Can you hear a buzzing sound? Those are bees searching for nectar. They take care to stay away from the birds since many of them like to snap them up with

their beaks. You may think that the bees do nothing but glide around flowers all day, buzzing happily, but they are really working very hard. Bees are very useful to plants because they help flowers to pollinate.

Birds and bees are both very helpful and without them I would not have so many flowers and fruits in my garden. Watch carefully and see how this happens. When a bee or small bird settles on a flower to drink nectar, a tiny bit of yellow powder called pollen gets stuck

on its body. Then it flies off to sip nectar from another flower, carrying the pollen dust with it. In this way the flowers get to exchange pollen and make seeds. This is the magic of nature.

Many other insects like butterflies and ants carry pollen from one flower to another and because they are so useful to plants, the flowers compete with each other to invite them. Some bring out bright red petals to attract birds and insects and others offer sweet nectar as a reward. The gulmohur tree produces bright orange-red flowers and tries to be more helpful by marking one petal in the flower with red dashes as if to say: 'this way for nectar'. Mynas and bulbuls

often ignore this invitation and munch on the little green buds instead.

My favourite tree in the garden is the tall jacaranda tree. It has beautiful blueish-purple flowers that are shaped like tiny tubes. The bee-eater, a tiny green

bird with a sharp beak, likes to perch on the jacaranda branches because there are many insects flying around the flowers. I love watching this bird as it flies around the garden catching insects. Like an ace pilot, it will take off from the branch and then swiftly catch a poor insect flying past in the air. Though they are such expert pilots, these birds build a nest in the ground by digging a long tunnel. There is a small

chamber at the end of the tunnel where the eggs can remain safely and the parent birds shoot into this underground nest at top speed.

While most birds look for food during the day, others like to come out only at night. Guess whoooo? If you see two yellow eyes shining in the dark, then you can be sure the spotted owlet has come out to hunt. Most owls look for food at night and rest in tree hollows during daylight. These birds eat insects, mice and lizards by catching them in

the dark. I have seen the owl quietly swooping down on a mouse that was scampering around in the garden. I am sure the mouse was told by its mother not to go out in the night but it did not listen. The owl swiftly made a dinner of it. When daylight streams into the garden, the owls hide in the hollow in the jacaranda tree and sometimes I see them staring at the cat with their bright yellow eyes. Then they decide the cat will not make a tasty meal and go back to sleep.

So you see, my garden is home to so many birds because it gives them plenty to eat and drink. Every garden, however small, will shelter birds and insects. In summer you will see so many birds sitting near the water tap or hosepipe, waiting for the water to come out. When I eat something in the garden, the birds will quickly come and pick up the crumbs as soon as I leave. Summer, winter or rains, there is always food for garden birds especially if it is a wild garden like mine with lots of shrubs and old trees.

The garden changes colour every season as the trees and plants turn from green to brown and back to green, but the birds stay in their favourite places and eat their favourite food.

# Chapter Two

*You and I can move around easily from* place to place, enjoying new kinds of food and scenery. You can go to the mountains or to the seaside or explore a jungle. Birds like to stay mostly in their own special place and this is called a habitat. There are some birds like ducks and geese that migrate from one habitat to another in search of food and they are happy to fly long distances to do so. Let us say goodbye for a little while to our garden birds and go and meet the birds that live near lakes and rivers.

The cat has decided to stay back in the garden because he is too lazy to walk in the muddy lanes around the lake. I think he is also a bit afraid of the jungle cats he might meet here. These wild cats are very clever at hiding in the scrub forest area and mostly come out to hunt at dusk when it is safe. My fat garden cat is no match for these expert catchers of field mice and rats.

Any large area of water always has some waterbirds roaming around in search of tasty food. Some birds walk around the edges of the lake, while others swim happily in the middle of the lake. Shall we see what each kind of bird is doing? We must walk very quietly and make sure we don't fall into a muddy ditch as we go close to the clump of reeds that grow around the lake.

The first bird that sees us is the paddy bird. This green, brown and yellow bird never says anything to anyone and keeps standing very still in one place, looking like a statue. The paddy bird eats frogs, small fish and insects and patiently waits for a long time to catch its food. It has a funny way of walking when it moves forward to catch a frog or insect it has spotted with its round, yellow eyes. One day I was walking happily near the lake

and suddenly a bird flew up right in front of my face. It was the paddy bird! I don't know who was more startled. The paddy bird muttered something rude about people disturbing its breakfast and then walked carefully down the squelchy mud to a safer spot.

The black-winged stilt wades in the shallow, marshy areas around the lake and its long legs enable it to walk fast in the muddy water to catch tadpoles and

insects easily. Even a very small pool of water will have a few of these pink-legged, black and white birds wading in it. Look out for them in village ponds. You will see them digging up insects and worms from the wet mud, their long legs supporting them like stilts. They are not afraid of people and pretend we don't exist even if we get quite close to them. Sometimes they move together and look like dancers matching their steps gracefully but look closely and you will find they are chasing some juicy aquatic insects.

The spotted sandpiper sings in a squeaky voice as it runs up and down on the edge of the lake, looking for food. This bird is a winter visitor and comes from colder regions for food and warmth to our country. When the brown-and-white spotted and streaked bird stands

still on the wet muddy ground, it is very difficult to see it even if you are standing very close.

The bright blue feathers of the small blue kingfisher cannot stay hidden and you will see this pretty bird mostly near ponds and rivers. Kingfishers do not eat just fish. They like tadpoles and insects too and can catch them easily with their long, pointed beak. They use their strong beaks to dig a long tunnel in the muddy riverbanks and nest in this safe, underground home. What fun to be able to dig a tunnel and build a secret room for yourself. You could put up a bookshelf, place a comfortable chair and read all day in this muddy home. But watch out when water in the river rises! You will have to swim out very fast, taking all your books with you.

Have you noticed that waterbirds have special beaks and feet that help them find food easily in the water? Ducks have webbed feet so that they can paddle swiftly from one part of the lake to another. Herons have long, sturdy legs and pointed beaks which enable them to catch lots of fish, frogs and swimming insects. Look at the spoonbill standing in the marshes. It has the best beak and never has to ask anyone

for a spoon when it begins to eat. This white bird keeps walking up and down in the shallow waters,

dragging its special spoon-shaped bill in the mud to pick up tiny fish, aquatic

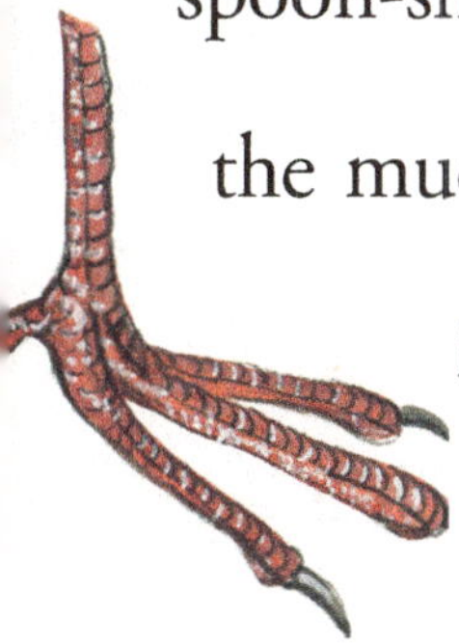

insects and tadpoles. Now you know why it is called a spoonbill! Imagine

having your own wonderful spoon to pick up dal and rice (my favourite food).

The white ibis has a bill that looks like a dangerous dagger, but this bird never harms anyone and only wants to eat seeds and tiny insects floating in the water.

Can you see that bird with a long snake-like neck? This is the snake-bird and it can chase fish even underwater at a great speed. With its long, pointed beak it will stab a fish quickly and pick it up. Sometimes I have seen the snake-bird catch a fish that is too big for it to eat. You know what it does then? It throws the fish in the air and then expertly catches it

by opening its beak wide to swallow the fish as it comes down. Can you do that? I certainly cannot. I tried to toss a pizza once and it fell right on my head.

Ducks only eat a small amount at a time but they seem to be eating all the time. You will see them swimming about on the lake, constantly looking for small insects and green vegetable matter in the

water. The spotbill duck has two big red spots on its beak and you can see it in many lakes and ponds, eating greedily all day long. The little duck you see is called dabchick and it swims very fast. It loves diving into the water to find food. Sometimes I have seen it running swiftly across the surface of the water and then diving as it chases a tadpole. This duck is always busy munching and reminds me of a greedy goblin from a fairy tale.

The spotbill duck and the dabchick can be seen throughout the year on the

lake but there are many other ducks that only come here in winter. These are called migratory birds since they fly in from faraway places and do not live here all the time like the resident birds. The pintail duck comes from Europe and northern Asia while the famous Siberian

crane flies all the way from Siberia to spend the winter at the Bharatpur National Park in Rajasthan. The greylag geese and bar-headed geese and many other birds also come from faraway, cold regions to our country during winter months. No one tells these migratory

birds the way to our country. They use their own special sense of direction to get here. Why do they fly so far? Why don't they stay at home and eat?

These birds live in very cold lands and it becomes very difficult to find food when the ground and lakes become frozen. That is why these clever birds leave their frozen homes as soon as winter sets in and fly to warmer lands. Here they find lots of sunshine all day and plenty to eat. They love green vegetable roots that grow in water, tender wheat shoots and aquatic insects. Most of these birds eat at night and doze with their heads tucked into their wings during the day, enjoying their sunny, winter holiday in India. I really admire these birds. Imagine having the courage to fly such a long distance with no maps or packed food. They just know they have to do it and take off. No tickets, no visa and no passports are needed for these amazing, long-distance travellers.

In winter, the sky above the lake has migratory birds flying around all

day long, honking and trumpeting. The flocks of ducks and geese form a V shape and then suddenly land on the water with a loud, drumming sound like horses running. The river tern watches them and flies away. This grey-and-white

bird loves to fly and hardly ever sits sill. It keeps looking down at the surface of the lake from above and suddenly dives down to catch a fish. This swift-flying bird is a cousin of the Artic tern, a bird that holds the world record of flying the longest distance. If ever there is an Olympics for birds then this little tern would win a gold medal every time.

The marsh harrier and the ring-tailed fishing eagle hunt above the water and scare all the birds swimming below. As soon as these two birds appear in the sky,

you will see the ducks quickly rushing to the other side of the lake. I have often seen the marsh harrier chasing the poor ducks all around the lake just for fun. These predator birds eat small birds, as well as fish and frogs, and sometimes

swoop down to catch a field mouse they have spotted with their sharp eyes.

Many waterbirds like to nest in the tall reeds that grow by the side of the lake. The birds look for a safe place in this wet and green jungle and often hide their nests very cleverly. The Indian moorhen and the purple moorhen both build their nests out of weeds and then put them on

the floating green plants. These two birds have large and ugly feet but these funny-looking feet help them walk easily on

floating plants like water lilies and water hyacinth as they search for food. When I see this clumsy bird walk across the lake, I always think of Charlie Chaplin doing his lopsided walk.

Let us leave the marshes and look at the birds swimming in the middle of the lake where the water is much deeper. The large bird you see is a grey pelican. These birds stay together in a group to catch fish. The birds have special bills that are like small fishing nets. The pelicans swim in a half circle and slowly drive the fish into one corner by flapping their wings. Then they pick them up quickly with their big beaks. Pelicans always look very serious as if thinking of important

matters all the time as they slowly swim from one side of the lake to another.

The flamingo too has an unusual beak. These tall, pink-legged white birds feed by putting their beaks upside down in the shallow water. The beak has a strainer inside and when the bird scoops

up a mouthful of mud, it enables it to sieve the tiny insects and seeds for the flamingo to eat. The birds move around the water very slowly and gracefully as if they were dancing and I can watch them for hours. They look like ballet dancers doing complicated steps to some beautiful music only they can hear.

The painted storks are large birds with powerful yellow beaks. These white birds have black stripes on their wings and splashes of pink that look as if someone had painted their wings, which is why they are called painted storks. They make a lot of noise as they fly about catching fish by dragging their long beaks in the water. They build untidy nests on trees near the water along with other waterbirds and they make a really loud noise all day. When the afternoon sun gets too hot for their newborn chicks, the painted storks spread their large wings

out like an umbrella over the nest to shade their chicks. A kind, thoughtful bird—but I am not sure if my children would like me to hold an umbrella over their heads all day long.

When many different kinds of waterbirds nest together on one tree, it is called a colony or a heronry. Every branch of the tree has two or three nests that belong to egrets, storks or herons. The birds keep landing on the tree and taking off, creating a lot of noise. When the chicks are born, they add to the noise too, since they are always screeching hungrily for food.

Look around the lake and you will see a tree shaking with birds as they flap their wings. These birds share the space on the tree happily like friends though

sometimes a mild argument breaks out if one of the birds lands on the wrong branch. There is so much noise around this tree and you wonder how each bird knows what the other is saying. It does look like a fun place to live though. Like a huge, friendly noisy hostel for birds. The lake is a friend to these waterbirds and gives them plenty of fish, frogs, insects, green vegetables and seeds to eat.

# Chapter Three

*We have seen birds that live in the* garden and on the lakes, so now let us go even further away to meet the birds that live in the forest. Birds really like living in forest areas because they have so many trees around them. They can choose safe places to build their nests and hide when we go looking for them. Before we walk into the forest let us see if there are any birds in the fields outside the forest area. The farmers use the land here to grow various crops like wheat, rice and corn. Birds know this and often fly in to eat whatever they like. Tender green shoots, seeds and even tiny leaves are all snapped up by the greedy birds.

Farmers put scarecrows in their fields to frighten the birds away but they do not really feel scared at all and eat to their heart's content.

The sarus crane never gets chased away by the farmers even when it is caught raiding their crops. People in the villages protect this bird because they

believe it has a very kind heart since it is devoted to its mate for life. You may be lucky enough to see this tallest bird of India dancing with its mate in the fields. They flap their wings and bow gracefully to each other as they sing out loudly in a trumpeting call as if playing a tune.

The grey partridge also calls out loudly to its mate and keeps repeating the same

'kattteer...katteeer' over and over again. I wonder if it is saying the same words again and again or has a new joke or something interesting to tell its mate. These plump, grey and brown birds are very clever at playing hide and seek and you will not be able to find them easily even if they are calling out near you. They walk about in the undergrowth looking for seeds and insects and do not like to fly much except when they are trying to escape from danger.

The cattle egret is a white bird you often see marching about in the fields. This bird sometimes rides on the backs of buffaloes and cows and quickly snaps up the insects that fly up when the animals step on the ground. The little egret often stays near its bigger cousin and they both like to follow the farmer when she ploughs her field and pick up the worms from

the freshly turned soil. Don't you think it is a clever idea? The farmer does all the hard work and the birds get to eat juicy worms. Very much like sitting on the sofa while your mother makes delicious food for you.

The red munias always eat and chat together. You will see flocks of these tiny birds making a huge racket as they

search for seeds to eat. The male munia is brown, as is the female, but during the breeding season he gets bright red feathers and looks very smart. I often watch him preening and looking around to see if all the other birds are admiring his glossy, new feathers.

The gentle spotted dove collects seeds by walking up and down on the forest paths. This dove has a soft call and says 'krroo...kookeroo' when it perches on the branches. There is another dove called the turtle dove that has brick-red

feathers on its back that gleam beautifully in the sunshine. Doves also like nesting near houses and when I hear doves call, I always think of long, lazy summer afternoons sitting under a tree in my garden. Doves never seem to quarrel.

The blue jay or the Indian roller has light blue and dark blue feathers and you will often see this bird sitting on telegraph poles near open fields. When it is sitting quietly, the blue jay looks like a drab brown bird. But wait. As soon as it takes off in the air, you will see its lovely blue feathers flash like a silken banner. The roller is very helpful to farmers since it eats a lot of insects that harm the crops.

The black drongo is an insect-eating bird too, and likes to chase after them in the air. This glossy-black bird is very brave and fights any bird that flies into its territory. Many non-fighting birds like doves and orioles like to nest near the drongo because they know that they will be protected by this fighter pilot bird. In fact, the Hindi name for this brave bird is 'kotwal' which means policeman.

The grey shrike hunts both in the fields and in the forest area. The bird has a sharp, hooked bill and wears a black mask over its eyes like a bandit. It is also

called the butcher bird since it hunts a large number of insects at a time and then sticks them on a thorn so that it can eat them later. The shrike is very careful when it flies to this secret store of insects and you will never be able to find out where they are hidden. Imagine having your own secret storehouse of yummy snacks that no one can find except for you.

Now let us leave the open fields and walk down the forest lane to search for hidden corners where we might see a few birds. The trees have many holes in their trunks and this is where woodpeckers, parakeets and owls usually nest. The rocky areas in the forest have many low shrubs and thorny plants. If you see a brown bird sitting quietly on a rock, looking like a big fat cat, then it is the Indian great horned owl. This big owl hunts for mice, lizards and frogs during the night and sleeps in a shady corner

during the day. I wonder what my cat will say when it meets this super owl of the bird world. I am sure it will quietly beat a dignified retreat.

The golden-backed woodpecker does not mind if you stand and watch it racing up and down the tree trunk, looking for insects in the bark. The bird has a powerful, pointed beak that can chip away the wood easily and that is how it makes a deep hole in the bark. Stand still in the forest and you will certainly hear a woodpecker hammering away

somewhere. It goes thak-thak-thak like a carpenter hammering nails on wood. I am sure a woodpecker could build little tables and chairs too if it needed some furniture for its nest. This cosy, safe woodpecker's nest is often used later by other birds too.

Did you notice how many of the waterbirds have long legs so that they can wade in the water easily? The birds that live mostly on trees have strong feet and claws that help them perch on the branches firmly. Those birds who like to run instead of flying have short, sturdy legs. All birds have special bills and feet depending on where they live and what they eat. So, you see, nature has thought of everything.

Sometimes the birds may fool you. Though the grey hornbill has a heavy strong bill that looks like a weapon, the bird eats mostly fruits, berries and small insects. It has a strange nesting habit. It finds a hollow in a tree and makes a nest with grass and twigs. Then the female bird settles down to lay her eggs in this hollow. The male bird plasters up the nest and leaves only a tiny window. The female stays locked up in this nest till the eggs have hatched. She is fed by the male bird through the little window. I have searched

for a long time for a grey hornbill's nest but never found one. Maybe you will be lucky enough to see this plastered nest on a tree trunk one day. Be careful and do not let the birds know you have seen their secret nest.

The tall trees in the forest have many bushes growing around them and the jungle fowl thinks this is the best place to hide in. The bright red, yellow and green bird is difficult to see since it scampers away very fast. The peacock and his several mates also run around fast in the scrub forest but are not shy at all. You will often see our beautiful national bird proudly displaying his feathers even in city parks and gardens. During the monsoon, you will hear them calling out loudly and sometimes it sounds like a cat mewing! It is a beautiful bird but its voice can shatter your eardrums.

Wherever they live, birds have to keep looking for food all the time. In the gardens and parks they have flowering shrubs and trees that give them plenty of food. Lakes and ponds give them fish to eat and trees in the forest offer them safe shelters. It is important that we make sure these lakes are free of garbage and plastic. If we dump waste material in the water, it gets polluted. Then the weeds and aquatic insects the birds eat

will vanish and there will be no food for them to eat.

Birds are a very important part of our natural environment and help plants to form seeds.

Birds have to work hard to build nests and search all over the place for building materials. In my garden they find plenty of twigs and soft grass and soft fur from my dogs! In the lake areas they use green plants and weeds, while in the forest they use dried grass and twigs. They have to carry all this building

material in their beaks but they do it quite happily as long as we do not harm them or their nests.

We must plant trees and shrubs wherever we can and look after them. The more green shelters there are around us, the better for us and for the birds.

Remember, they are our friends. They eat up harmful insects and help the farmers. They sing songs for us all day. Can you imagine a world without birds? What would the gardens, the lakes or the forests be like without them? When you see a bird flying freely in the sky, you learn that you can be brave and strong even when you are a tiny bundle of feathers.

# Helping Birds

*Put water out in clay containers during* summer months. It is great fun to watch birds bathing, preening their feathers and chattering to each other.

Put bird seed near the container and offer them a free meal.

If you are good with your hands, build a small wooden house and hang it on a tree. If you are lucky, a bird might come and nest in it.

Plant a few flowering shrubs near your house and wait for the birds to arrive.

Plant trees like guava, mango and jamun if you can. Birds like to gather on these trees.